'Twas the Day Before Zoo Day

By Catherine Ipcizade

Illustrated by Ben Hodson

'Twas the day before Zoo Day, when all 'round the park,
the creatures felt restless and wished it were dark.
Zoo keepers all scurried to get things prepared.
Flamingos stood antsy on one leg and stared.

Soon the kids would arrive; their cameras they'd bring.

The monkeys—they practiced to dance and to sing.

Kids like to watch monkeys, and everyone knows,

that monkeys, like children, hang down from their toes.

The trainers begged llamas to please be polite,

"Don't go around spitting. It's just not all right!"

Giraffes used their blue tongues to drink and to slurp.

"We might drool sometimes, but we try not to burp."

The rhinos were lazy and didn't roam far.

Did you know rhinos weigh as much as a car?

And the African meerkats watched from their dens,

while nibbling on bugs, huddled close to their friends.

When out in the swamp there arose such a shriek,

the toucans took cover and squawked with their beaks.

For a gator mistook a bee for a fly,

he opened his jaws but got stung in the eye.

While out in the dirt, naughty elephants rolled,

not listening at all to what they'd been told.

They frolicked in mud to cool down from the sun.

Their trunks became sprinklers and soaked everyone.

The lions just slept, not a care to be found.

Their heads on their paws, they nestled the ground.

When you're king of the jungle, these things are okay.

So they sleep and they sleep—20 hours each day.

Zebras stood griping, not happy at all.

Their black and white stripes had gotten quite dull.

They wished to be spotted, with big polka dots,
but zebras aren't meant to be covered with spots.

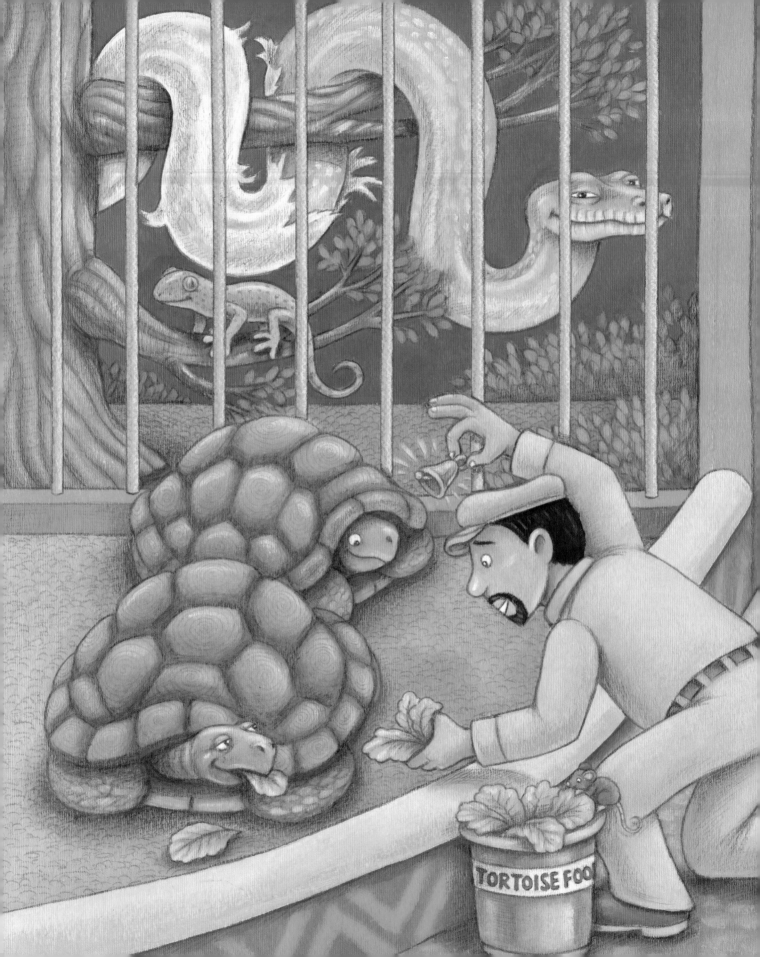

Trainers coaxed turtles gently out of their shells,
they cleaned up the doodoo and rang mealtime bells.
The snakes shed their skin while the geckos took cover.
The antelope grazed and played with each other.

With big wooly paws and eyes like the night,
the black bears look scary and cause a fright.
But they really like frolicking out in the sun.
It's true they roar loudly, but mostly for fun.

With a flick of a hose and a soft, sturdy broom,
the elephants were bathed and looked shiny and groomed.
They knew they were ready for tomorrow's zoo day,
when the children would come to point, watch, and play.

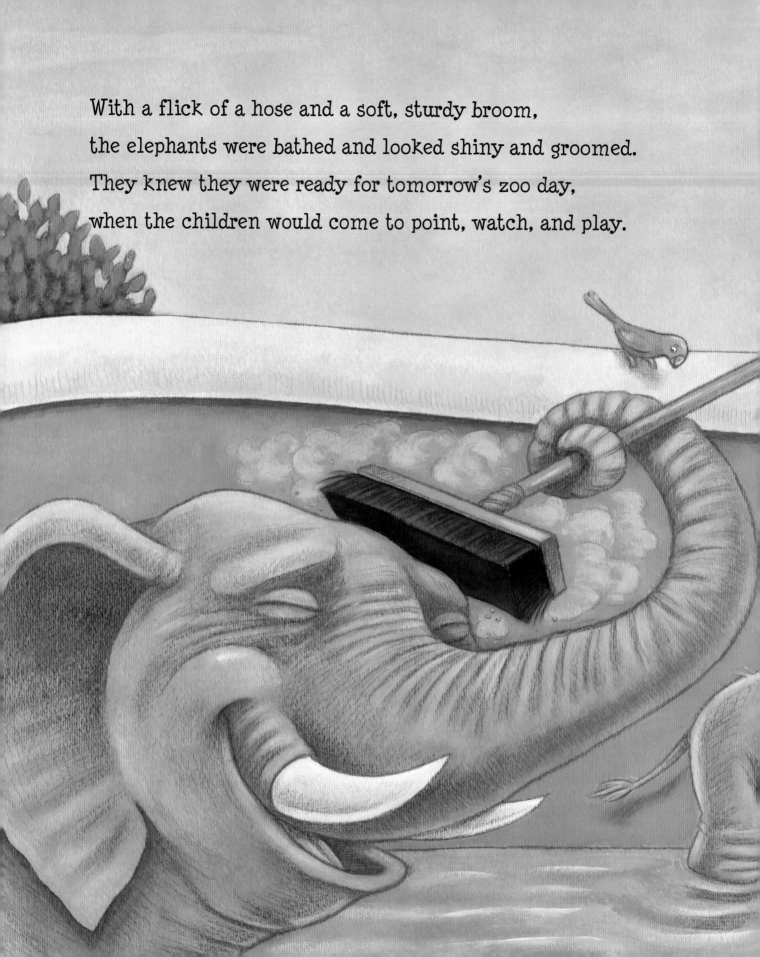

Then the sun went down, and the keepers went home,
and the animals stayed at the zoo on their own.
Some closed sleepy eyes, while others awoke.
Daddies shushed kids to sleep while they whispered and joked.

Then parents and babies prepared for the rush,
as kids filtered out of the yellow school bus.
And a mama gorilla whispered in the light,
"It's Zoo Day my baby, hold on to me tight."

For Creative Minds

Adaptation Matching Activity

Match the correct animal to its adaptation to survive in its habitat.

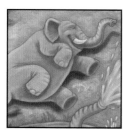

1. _____

2. _____

3. _____

4. _____

5. _____

a. Black Bear

My long, curved claws and long tongue help me grab insects.

b. Snake

I have lots of bones so I can easily bend and slither around.

c. Zebra

My black and white stripes help to hide me in the tall grass.

d. Turtle

I have a thick shell to protect me from predators.

e. Giraffe

I have a long neck to eat leaves high in the trees.

f. Monkey

I have a tail that I use like a hand to grab and to hold onto things.

_____ 6.

g. Elephant

I use my trunk to drink water and to feel things around me.

_____ 7.

h. Alligator

My eyes are high on my head so I can see when I'm in the water.

_____ 8.

i. Gorilla

My thumbs help me to grab food and to hold onto things.

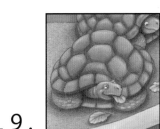

_____ 9.

j. Toucan

I have a strong beak to break open nuts and fruit to eat.

_____ 10.

Animal Fun Facts

animal	class	babies called	weight at birth	family group	eat
Black Bears	Mammals	Cubs	< 1 lb.	Solitary	Omnivore
Elephants	Mammals	Calves	250 lb.	Herd	Herbivore
Flamingos	Birds	Chicks	3 oz.	Colony	Omnivore
Giraffes	Mammals	Calves	150 lb.	Herd	Herbivore
Gorillas	Mammals	Babies	3 - 4 lb.	Band	Herbivore
Lions	Mammals	Cubs	1 $\frac{1}{2}$ lb.	Pride	Carnivore
Llamas	Mammals	Crias	20 - 30 lb.	Family	Herbivore
Meerkats	Mammals	Pups	2 oz.	Mob or Gang	Omnivore
Rhinos	Mammals	Calves	88 - 144 lb.	Crash	Herbivore
Zebras	Mammals	Foals	55 lb.	Herd	Herbivore

Zoo keepers

People have all kinds of different jobs such as policemen, firemen, doctors, nurses, or veterinarians. Some are teachers and some work at home caring for young children. Zoo keepers, like the man and the woman in the book, care for animals at zoos and aquariums. Unlike veterinarians who usually work with individual animals once or twice a year or when they are sick, zoo keepers can work with animals all the time. Zoo keepers are scientists who:

- Feed the animals and make sure they get their vitamins.

- Clean the area where the animals live.

- Know the animals very well, just like you know a pet dog or cat. They can tell if an animal is getting sick or doesn't feel well.

- Give animals basic checkups. Sometimes they have to train the animals to stand still while being examined. Other animals may have to go to sleep to be examined.

- Make sure that the animals keep busy and get enough exercise.

- Help with conservation of endangered or threatened animals.

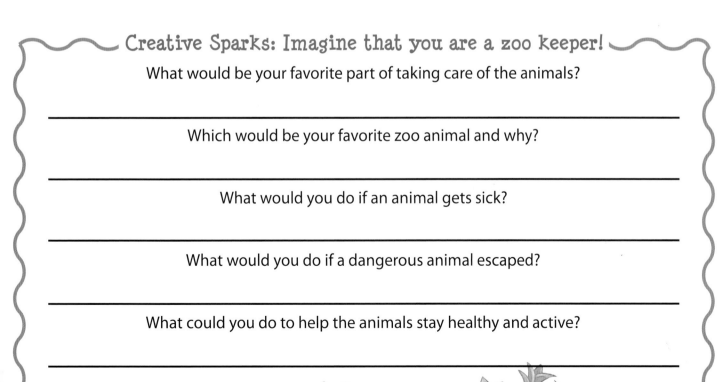

Creative Sparks: Imagine that you are a zoo keeper!

What would be your favorite part of taking care of the animals?

_____

Which would be your favorite zoo animal and why?

_____

What would you do if an animal gets sick?

_____

What would you do if a dangerous animal escaped?

_____

What could you do to help the animals stay healthy and active?

_____

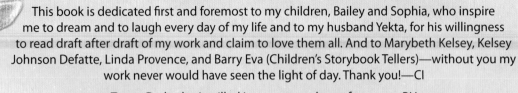

This book is dedicated first and foremost to my children, Bailey and Sophia, who inspire me to dream and to laugh every day of my life and to my husband Yekta, for his willingness to read draft after draft of my work and claim to love them all. And to Marybeth Kelsey, Kelsey Johnson Defatte, Linda Provence, and Barry Eva (Children's Storybook Tellers)—without you my work never would have seen the light of day. Thank you!—CI

To my Dad, who instilled in me a great love of nature—BH

Thanks to Norah Farnham, Zoo Keeper, of the American Association of Zoo Keepers, for verifying the accuracy of the information in this book.

Publisher's Cataloging-In-Publication Data

Ipcizade, Catherine.
'Twas the day before zoo day / by Catherine Ipcizade ; illustrated by Ben Hodson.

p. : col. ill. ; cm.

Summary: In an adaptation of the children's classic, 'Twas the Night Before Christmas, preparations are under way for Zoo Day. But things aren't going according to plan. Does it all work out? Will the zookeepers end up spending the night at the zoo? Will Zoo Day go off without a hitch, or will the dancing monkeys take over? "For Creative Minds" section includes animal matching activities and riddles.
Interest age level: 003-007.
Interest grade level: P-2.
ISBN: 978-1-934359-08-2 (hardcover)
ISBN: 978-1-934359-24-2 (pbk.)

1. Zoo animals--Juvenile fiction. 2. Zoos--Juvenile fiction.
3. Zoo animals--Fiction. 4. Zoos--Fiction. 5. Stories in rhyme.
I. Hodson, Ben. II. Title. III. Title: Zoo day

PZ10.3.I63 Tw 2008[E]   2007935083

Printed in China

Sylvan Dell Publishing
976 Houston Northcutt Blvd., Suite 3
Mt. Pleasant, SC 29464